This Coloring Book

Belongs

To:

CHILDHOOD
CANCER
AWARENESS

FIGHT LIKE
AILANI

KURE FEST

#CURE

#cure
4ailani

KICKING CANCER BUTT.

HOSPITAL
BMT
CAR-T CELL
Chemo
cure4
ailani

Johns Hoppkins Children's Hospital
beads of courage

Honored
Heroes
COOL
KIDZ!
#FIGHT
4
AILANI
JOJO
BRAVE!
ZOEY
MADDI

HELP CURE CANCER ONCE AND 4 ALL
DONATION
#CURE4
AILANI

curecc
#rallykid
ailani
cure

CURE
CHILDHOOD CANCER

BRAVE
#TEAM
AILANI
BSU
BSU

AACS
#cure
4ailani

HONORED HERO

#CURE

AEROANGEL

#cure4ailani

Made in the USA
Middletown, DE
06 May 2024

53933961R00031